Discovering Norse Mythology

Heroes and Villains OF NORSE MYTHOLOGY

Don Nardo

ReferencePoint Press

San Diego, CA

Printed in the United States

For more information, contact:
ReferencePoint Press, Inc.
PO Box 27779
San Diego, CA 92198
www.ReferencePointPress.com

LIBRARY OF CONGRESS CATALOGING-IN-PUBLICATION DATA

Names: Nardo, Don, 1947- author.
Title: Heroes and villains of Norse mythology / by Don Nardo.
Description: San Diego, CA : ReferencePoint Press, Inc., 2025. | Series: Discovering norse mythology | Includes bibliographical references and index.
Identifiers: LCCN 2024049113 (print) | LCCN 2024049114 (ebook) | ISBN 9781678210342 (library binding) | ISBN 9781678210359 (ebook)
Subjects: LCSH: Mythology, Norse--Juvenile literature.
Classification: LCC BL860 .N266 2025 (print) | LCC BL860 (ebook) | DDC 293/.13--dc23/eng/20250103
LC record available at https://lccn.loc.gov/2024049113
LC ebook record available at https://lccn.loc.gov/2024049114

CONTENTS

Courage in the Face of Suffering

Gunnar Hammandarson glanced out the window of his farmhouse and was distressed to see his fellow villager Thorgeir Otkelsson and five of Thorgeir's relatives and friends approaching. All were well armed with swords and spears. And Gunnar knew they were coming to kill him. He did not want to fight them, for he was a peaceful individual at heart and wanted only to get along with his neighbors. But he felt he had no choice. His honor had been questioned, and in his society a man's honor had to be defended even if it meant fighting and dying or killing someone else.

Gunnar's and Thorgeir's society was that of the tenth-century Icelandic Vikings. Also called the Norse, the Vikings were a robust and resilient people who inhabited Scandinavia and Iceland during the mid-medieval period. From shortly before 800 to shortly after 1000 CE, groups of Vikings fairly regularly attacked the coasts of England, Ireland, France, and other parts of western Europe. They also frequently fought among themselves.

Gunnar Hammandarson
A legendary Icelandic Viking known for his courage, strength, and fighting skills

And this is why, on this day, Gunnar and Thorgeir were about to meet each other in a fight to the death. Knowing Gunnar's reputation as a courageous—some would say invincible—warrior, Thorgeir had brought along extra men. According to *Njal's Saga*, an anonymous thirteenth-century Icelandic narrative, no Viking

Thorgeir Otkelsson
A neighbor of Gunnar Hammandarson's who questions his honor and attacks him

fighter had ever been Gunnar's equal. It was said that he was so powerful and agile that he could jump his own height in full armor. And he swung his sword so swiftly it looked like he was using three swords at once.

The dispute between Gunnar and Thorgeir had started small. It had been instigated by Gunnar's headstrong and mischievous wife, Hallgerdur. Behind her husband's back, she had ordered her slave to steal some items from Thorgeir's home, and the slave had been caught in the act. Per Viking custom, the embarrassed Gunnar had offered Thorgeir financial compensation. But not only had Thorgeir refused, he had called Gunnar's honor into question.

For that reason, as the five men approached Gunnar's house, he collected his weapons and went out to fight them. *Njal's Saga* states that Thorgeir, wielding a spear, attacked Gunnar, who swiftly broke the weapon in half. In that instant, "Gunnar saw another man come within reach of his sword and struck him his death blow and then seized the spear in both hands. Thorgeir Otkelsson had meanwhile moved in close, with his sword at the ready. Gunnar turned toward him quickly. . . . He thrust his spear through him and lifted him up high and threw him out into the river."[1]

Although Gunnar managed to defeat the attackers, a few years later another feud led fourteen warriors to assault his home. At first, he used arrows to kill several of them. But then his bowstring broke. Turning toward Hallgerdur, he asked her to give him a lock of her hair with which to fashion a new string. For reasons unknown, however, she refused. And though he fought heroically, the attackers eventually prevailed and slew him.

Mythical Good Guys and Bad Guys

Gunnar Hammandarson remains one of the most memorable human heroes of Norse mythology. That world-famous collection of tales also features numerous stories about the Norse gods and their interactions with people. But the Vikings remembered human

heroes of their distant and recent past fondly, and because of that, they eagerly passed on the stories about them to each new generation. Among the other admirable humans in those stories was Sigurd, famous for slaying a dragon, and the dashing outlaw Egil Skallagrimsson, who was also a talented poet. In addition, universally loved and celebrated among the Vikings was the legendary warrior-king Ragnar Lothbrok, known for the fearless way he faced a gruesome death.

Most of the Norse gods were also seen as heroic figures. As the late, great scholar of Norse civilization and myths H.R.E. Davidson said, those beings were in a sense "humans writ large." They possessed strong values and would rather die, she pointed out, "than surrender those values."[2] This quality was hugely admired by the Vikings. Among the most revered of those deities were the stalwart scholar-warrior Odin and his intrepid son Thor, who wielded a hammer that could pulverize mountain peaks.

As might be expected, the Norse myths also feature an array of villains. Particularly famous among them was Loki, the deity of deceit, often called the trickster, who repeatedly betrayed his fellow gods. His monstrous offspring—including an enormous wolf, huge serpent, and witchlike queen of the underworld—were also villains in those tales. And so were giants, dragons, zombies, and others.

Almost Obsessed with Heroism

The theme of heroes versus villains was therefore pervasive in Norse mythology. In fact, the Vikings were almost obsessed with the very concept of heroism, although they tended to define it differently than people do today. In their view, as the late, renowned historian Edith Hamilton explained,

> the power of good is shown not by triumphantly conquering evil, but by continuing to resist evil while facing certain defeat. . . . The hero in one of the Norse myths who laughs aloud while his foes cut his heart out . . . shows himself superior to his conquerors. He says to them, in effect, "you can do nothing to me because I do not care what you do." They kill him, but he dies undefeated.[3]

To the Norse, dishonorable, villainous characters, both real and mythical, were just one more unpleasant reality of life. Others included disease, old age, and growing enough food to sustain themselves in the cold, mountainous regions of extreme northern Europe. One way that the Vikings countered life's hardships was by developing the bold, defiant outlook that Hamilton described. In their eyes, she said, "to live is to suffer and the only solution of the problem of life is to suffer with courage."[4] This singular attitude is duly reflected in the Norse myths, in which the heroes regularly personify that steadfast refusal to be defeated by life's difficulties.

Thor Versus the Giants

Standing more than 40 feet, almost 15 meters, tall, Hrungnir was one of the largest of the Jotnar, the race of beings who dwelled in Jotunheim. The land of the giants, it was the biggest of the many continent-like realms making up Yggdrasil, the World Tree. According to the Vikings and the tales composing their collected myths, the entire universe was contained within that enormous structure.

The conceited, brutish Hrungnir was the king of a large section of Jotunheim. But he had long dreamed of having even more power. In particular, he wanted to take over another important realm of the great tree—Asgard, the home the Aesir, the Norse gods. Like most giants, Hrungnir envied and despised those deities. He hoped someday to kill their leader, Odin, often called the All-Father. But the giant-king knew that doing so would not be easy, for Odin's son, Thor, the god of thunder, was often in Asgard. And Hrungnir profoundly feared Thor. This was because that burly divinity wielded the most destructive weapon in the world—Mjolnir, a hammer that could destroy an entire mountain in a single blow.

Hrungnir
A giant who tried but failed to take over Asgard, the realm of the gods

Therefore, Hrungnir waited until he heard that Thor was traveling somewhere far from Asgard. The giant then contacted Odin and claimed to want to pay him a peaceful visit. The All-Father, who feared nothing, accepted and took the huge visitor on a tour of one of Asgard's largest halls. According to mythologist Kevin Crossley-Holland, Hrungnir said to Odin, "This hall! Do you think it's big?" "Well," said Odin, "it does have five hundred and forty doors." "Piddling," the giant bellowed. "You think it's big and I say it's small. I'll pick it up and carry it home with me."[5]

Hrungnir quickly said he was just joking. But Odin could tell that the visitor had meant it. This was proved when, only a few days after leaving Asgard, the giant returned, expecting to launch a surprise attack on the gods. But this plan failed miserably. Hrungnir managed to enter the great hall and proceeded to insult and threaten the gathered gods. At that moment, however, Thor appeared, having come home earlier than expected.

The Vikings believed that Yggdrasil, or the World Tree, contained the entire universe.

Almost instantly, Hrungnir's demeanor changed from one of arrogance to abject terror. Panicking, he hurled his only weapon—a big whetstone (a stone normally used for sharpening tools)—at the thunder god. But in Crossley-Holland's words, Thor had already released mighty Mjolnir. "After it had smashed the whetstone, Thor's hammer crashed against Hrungnir's skull and smashed it into smithereens. The giant collapsed, stone dead on the stony ground."[6]

Thor's Crucial Rivalry with the Jotnar

Hrungnir's hatred of the Aesir was nothing new for most of Jotunheim's residents. Untold numbers of centuries before he was born, other giants had attacked Asgard. But usually well before they could do any harm to the gods' palaces, an incredibly lethal force had stopped them.

That formidable force took the form of Thor, who employed his famous hammer to dispatch such interlopers. Just as most giants despised the Aesir, Thor distrusted and disliked most of the Jotnar. That attitude, coupled with the use of murderous Mjolnir,

This picture shows Thor and his hammer, Mjolnir, which could destroy an entire mountain in a single blow.

Thor's Family, Home, and Appearance

Over the centuries, Thor has been one of the most important, famous, and popular of the Norse gods. His physical appearance and public image were unique and arresting. According to the late, noted scholar of Norse civilization H.R.E. Davidson, in medieval writings and artworks he most often appeared as

> a burly, red-headed man, immensely strong, with a huge appetite, blazing eyes, and a beard, full of enormous vitality and power. He could increase his strength by wearing a special belt of might. Other prize possessions of his were his great gloves, enabling him to grasp and shatter rocks, the chariot drawn by goats which took him across the sky, and his hammer. This last was regarded as the greatest of all the treasures of Asgard.

H.R.E. Davidson, *Scandinavian Mythology*. New York: Peter Bedrick, 1986, pp. 59–60.

gave Thor a reputation as both a giant killer and the chief protector of Asgard. Moreover, he not only defended that realm and its divine residents but also at times visited Jotunheim, where a number of giants tangled with him and lost.

In part, the medieval Vikings viewed those tales in which the heroic gods battled the villainous giants as entertainment. During northern Europe's many cold winter nights, it was common for extended family and friends to gather around a large fire. Typically, at least some of the evening would be devoted to listening to a skald—a Norse storyteller. He would recite various tales about the exploits of gods, giants, and other inhabitants of the World Tree.

The stories went beyond mere entertainment, however. The Norse recognized that the myths often had deeper meanings about the nature of life and the universe. In that regard, Odin, Thor, and the other Aesir personified civilization, order, and justice. In contrast, the Jotnar symbolized barbarism, chaos, and injustice.

To the Vikings, therefore, when Thor opposed and at times slew giants, he was trying to maintain the natural order of things. According to H.R.E. Davidson, "The power of the thunder god, symbolized by his hammer, extended over all that had to do with the well-being of the community." Indeed, without Thor and his signature weapon, "Asgard could no longer be guarded against the giants."[7] And if the Jotnar overran Asgard, the gods might lose their overall military mastery of the known world.

In the eyes of the Norse, such a loss would be disastrous for them as well. After all, they firmly believed that the Aesir and giants were real, as was the World Tree and its many realms. It is no wonder, then, that from an early age members of each new Norse generation eagerly absorbed all the stories about Thor's rivalry with the giants.

How Thor Got His Hammer

One of the most popular of those tales explained how the thunder god got his enormously destructive weapon—Mjolnir—in the first place. It began when the trickster god, Loki, paid a visit to his friend Brok, a resident of Svartalfheim, the underground realm of the dwarfs. Within this realm existed a vast subterranean complex of mines and forges. Over time, the hardworking dwarfs had built a reputation for being innovative and skilled blacksmiths and craftspeople.

Svartalfheim
The realm of the dwarfs, who were known for their inventiveness and craftsmanship

After Loki and Brok exchanged pleasantries, they got into an argument over which of the dwarfs produced the most exquisite objects. Brok insisted that it was his brother, Sindre. But Loki contended that the sons of the dwarf Ivald were the finest craftworkers. Hoping to resolve the issue, the two made a bet. A few weeks hence, they agreed, each would present some dwarf-made artifacts to Odin and the other gods. The gods would decide whose work was the finest—and thus who would win the wager.

When that day arrived, Loki gave Odin a magnificent spear made by Ivald's sons, a weapon guaranteed never to miss its mark. Then Brok confidently stepped forward and handed Thor a finely crafted hammer. It was called Mjolnir, meaning "lightning," the dwarf explained, and it was the most powerful weapon in the

A Giant's Scheme to Slay Thor

Many giants feared Thor and his hammer. And more than a few of them wanted to find some way to kill the thunder god. One of them, named Geirrod, realized that the only realistic way to slay Thor was to somehow separate him from the hammer. To do that, Geirrod first captured the god of deceit, Loki. The giant threatened to starve the trickster to death in a dungeon if he did not persuade Thor to enter Jotunheim without his hammer. Fearful, Loki lied to Thor, telling him that an attractive giantess, Gjalp, wanted to mate with him. But she would not meet with him if he was carrying his hammer. Thor initially fell for that story. But luckily for him another giantess, Grior, who genuinely admired him, tipped him off about the plot. She also gave him a magical staff and a pair of iron gloves, which came in handy when he reached Jotunheim. Acting on Geirrod's orders, Gjalp tried to drown the god in a river. But Thor used the staff to vault himself out of the turbulent waters. He then hurried to Geirrod's hall, put on the gloves, and hurled a blob of red-hot metal at the giant, killing him instantly.

universe. Not only could it smash an entire mountain into pebbles, Brok said, but after it had been tossed, it would always fly back into the thrower's hand.

Captivated, Thor grasped the hammer and swung it around a bit. Immediately, bolts of lightning shot out of it and up into the sky, igniting enormous peals of thunder. As the late mythologist Hamilton W. Mabie remarked, the awestruck gods "gathered around, and passed the hammer from one to the other, saying that it would be their greatest protection against their enemies."[8] As might be expected, to Loki's dismay, Brok won the bet.

The Day Thor Wore a Dress

After that Thor took the mighty Mjolnir with him wherever he went. And with that devastating weapon, he sent untold numbers of giants to their graves. As a result, Thor came to highly treasure the hammer. It was not surprising, therefore, that when one day it came up missing, he was deeply troubled.

Thor's first thought at that moment was to alert the other Aesir, and the first of their number that he told was Loki. Mjolnir's loss was certainly concerning, Loki agreed, because without it Asgard was less safe from the Jotnar. After discussing the matter, the two concluded that most likely the thief was one of those giants. Loki offered to travel to Jotunheim and there try to determine which giant had swiped the hammer.

Thor did not then realize that Loki secretly suspected who the thief was—a giant named Thrym. Loki had known Thrym for many years, and the giant had occasionally mentioned that he would love to get his hands on Mjolnir. Sure enough, when Loki confronted him, Thrym readily admitted to stealing the weapon. There was only one way that Thor would ever get the hammer back, Thrym told Loki. Namely, Odin and the other gods had to allow Thrym to marry the beautiful Freya, goddess of love.

Thrym
A giant who stole Thor's hammer and demanded to marry Freya, the goddess of love

When Loki returned to Asgard and reported what Thrym had said, Odin, Thor, Freya, and the other Aesir were outraged. There was no way that Freya was going to wed Thrym, they all agreed. But they must, at all costs, retrieve Thor's hammer. It was Heimdall, the deity who guarded the bridge linking Asgard to the human realm of Midgard, who proposed a plan designed to do just that. The gods should pretend to go along with the marriage, Heimdall said. But instead of Freya traveling to Jotunheim for the wedding, Thor should go instead, disguised as the goddess. Once there, he could rip Mjolnir from Thrym's grasp.

Thor was decidedly unhappy about dressing in women's clothes. But he reasoned that it would be worthwhile if it allowed him to get his beloved hammer back. He and Loki, also disguised as a woman, journeyed to Thrym's castle and mingled with the hundreds of guests. As part of the wedding celebration, the guests were invited to partake in a feast. So tempted was Thor (still disguised as Freya) by the delicious-smelling dishes that he proceeded to consume enormous helpings of beef, lamb, and other meats. Thrym was aghast at this display. According to modern storyteller Neil Gaiman, he told the disguised Loki, "Amazing! I've never seen any woman eat so ravenously!"[9]

The giant, Thrym, stole Thor's hammer and would only return it in exchange for permission to marry Freya, goddess of love, pictured here.

A little while later, Thrym announced that it was time for the ceremony. Hoping to impress his bride with the immense power he possessed, he placed Mjolnir in the lap of the person he thought was Freya. Thor responded immediately. He stood and struck Thrym only once, Gaiman writes, "but once was all it took. The ogre fell to the straw-covered floor and did not rise again. All the giants and ogres fell beneath Thor's hammer, the guests at the wedding that was not meant to be."[10]

Only after he had littered the hall with mangled bodies did Thor notice that he had forgotten to remove his disguise before going into battle. In the years that followed, he was destined to slay numerous other giants. But never would he kill as many as he did on the day he wore a dress.

CHAPTER TWO

Troubles with Two-Faced Loki

Odin, Loki, and several other members of the Aesir gathered in a meadow near the All-Father's palace, situated near the center of Asgard. Not long before, the gods had fought a war with another group of deities—the Vanir. And although a peace treaty had been signed, Odin was nervous about the future. During the conflict, the Vanir had easily entered and ransacked Asgard because it had no defensive wall. So Odin now made the case that such a wall was needed.

By sheer coincidence, the next day a large, muscular man riding a large, muscular horse, arrived and introduced himself to the gods. He said he was a master mason and offered to build a huge, strong wall around the entire kingdom. Loki asked his price. The stranger replied that he wanted the hand of the love goddess Freya in marriage.

A Devious Plan

In private, the gods discussed the matter, and all agreed that having Freya marry the mason was out of the question. But Loki, well known for being devious, had an idea. According to the late mythologist Brian Branston's version of the tale, Loki argued that the gods should agree to the marriage—but not without conditions. As Branston tells it, Loki suggested the gods "set such hard conditions that he won't be able to fulfill them, and then we can slide out of our side of the bargain."[11] Odin and the others decided that Loki's idea made sense and hired the mason to do the job.

Svadilfari
The horse belonging to the master mason who offered to construct a defensive wall around Asgard

The deal, brokered by Loki, called for the man to complete the project in one year. For a while, the mason's slow pace suggested that he would never finish on time. But his pace increased dramatically once he began using his powerful horse, Svadilfari, to transport and lift the stones. When the last day of the year arrived, it appeared the builder would finish on time after all.

Odin was livid. He ordered Loki to make sure that did not happen. Fearful of Odin's wrath, Loki—a skilled shape-shifter—transformed himself into a mare. In that guise he lured the

Odin rides his much-loved horse, Sleipnir. Sleipnir was a magical beast with eight legs, as depicted here.

lovestruck Svadilfari away into a nearby forest. As a result of Loki's interference, the mason missed his deadline—ending his hopes of marrying Freya.

Clever Loki had saved the day, but not without suffering his own insult. After Svadilfari caught up with his new love interest, he impregnated the mare. A few months later, Branston wrote, Loki "gave birth to a foal. It was grey and had eight legs. Odin took possession of him and called him Sleipnir."[12] In this way, Loki avoided being punished for the bad deal he had made. And because Odin came to love Sleipnir, Loki remained on good terms with the All-Father—at least for a while.

The Archvillain of Norse Folklore?

Loki's tendency to cheat, mislead, and lie, coupled with his boldness, cunning, and shape-shifting abilities, make him unlike any other being in the Norse myths. H.R.E. Davidson called him "perhaps the most outstanding character among the [Norse] gods, the chief actor in the most amusing stories, and the motivating force in a large number of [sinister] plots. . . . He is evidently an ambivalent [two-sided] character, neither wholly good nor wholly bad."[13]

Indeed, even a cursory glance at the collection of Norse myths shows that Loki is distinctly two-faced. In some myths he is congenial with his fellow deities and comes to their aid. Yet in other tales he betrays and schemes against them. This is why the Vikings called him both the trickster and the god of deceit. From a modern viewpoint, moreover, he is frequently seen as the archvillain of Norse folklore.

If Loki could not always be trusted, why would the other Aesir have put up with him for so long? Various experts have weighed in on this question. Edith Hamilton noted that Odin appears to have had a special relationship with Loki. "Wherever he came, trouble followed. He continually involved the gods in difficulties and dangers, but he was allowed to come freely to Asgard because for some reason never explained, Odin had sworn brotherhood with him."[14]

Loki's Ultimate Fate

After the other members of the Aesir found out about Loki's hand in Baldur's tragic death, they immediately sought to take him into custody. But they soon realized that he had fled Asgard. An exhaustive search followed, until they caught up with him on a secluded mountain peak on the far side of Jotunheim. There the trickster had been living in a small hunter's cottage near a waterfall that flowed into a stream. As the Aesir approached, Loki jumped into the stream and transformed himself into a fish. That ruse failed, however, because Odin and the others had expected him to shape-shift to avoid detection.

After capturing him, they took him to a cave inside a mountain in Asgard and bound him in heavy iron chains. They placed a poisonous snake directly above his head, and that reptile dripped its caustic venom onto his face several times a day, causing him agonizing pain. Eventually, however, a prophecy saying that the forces of evil would destroy the Aesir came to pass. On the day of that fateful battle—called Ragnarok—Loki broke free, rushed out, and joined the evil ones. A few hours later he died in the fighting, in which Odin and most of the other gods perished as well.

University of California, Berkeley, scholar John Lindow suggests a possible reason for this. Namely, Odin might have hoped to control the trickster's innate deceitful and destructive urges. "It seems likely to me," Lindow writes, "that Odin entered into blood brotherhood with Loki in an attempt to head off future mortal conflict with him. If so, Odin failed."[15]

Idunn's Special Apples

Indeed, most modern experts on Norse mythology agree that Odin gave Loki far too much latitude. Possibly partly due to that leniency, they say, the trickster's transgressions got more and more serious over time. One of the major warning signs of that progression was when Loki decided to aid the kidnapper of a fellow deity. The deity's name was Idunn. Idunn oversaw the fertility and life cycles of living things, including the rejuvenation of plants, animals, and even the gods. In fact, the Aesir were not innately immortal, like the Greek gods. Idunn periodically gave Odin and the others special apples that kept them in the peak of health and extended their lifetimes. Without the fruit she provided them, noted scholar of Norse culture Daniel McCoy explains, "old age began to creep up on the gods. Their skin wrinkled, their hair turned white and started to fall out, and their bodies became frail and diseased."[16]

The trouble with Idunn began when Odin, Loki, and Hoenir, god of silence and spirituality, went on a hunting trip in one of Asgard's deep forests. After a long, arduous hike, the three stopped to slaughter an ox, cook it, and eat supper. During the meal, the three noticed an unusually large eagle sitting on a tree branch directly above them. The eagle spoke up, telling the gods that it was quite hungry. And then it suddenly swooped down and grabbed the steak from Loki's plate.

Outraged, Loki clutched his walking staff and swung it at the oversized bird, which reacted by seizing him and carrying him off. "The eagle didn't soar," as Kevin Crossley-Holland tells it. "No, he skimmed just a few feet above the ground for miles and miles so that the trickster's ankles and knees, shoulders, and elbows were grazed by thorns and thistles, and scraped and bloodied by outcrops of rock."[17]

Loki repeatedly screamed for help and pleaded with the eagle to release him. In response, the creature said that it would do so only if Loki agreed to lure the goddess Idunn and her magical apples away from Asgard and into Jotunheim. That remark made Loki wonder if the eagle was actually a giant who had shape-shifted into a bird. And sure enough, when the trickster voiced that suspicion, the eagle admitted he was really a giant named Thiazi.

Thiazi

A giant who transformed himself into an eagle and abducted the goddess Idunn

Loki Lives Up to His Nickname

Loki knew it was wrong to agree to Thiazi's condition for releasing him. But the god of deceit once more lived up to that nickname.

The two made a deal. A few days later Loki tricked Idunn into placing her apples in a bag and carrying them into a wooded area of Jotunheim. There Thiazi, having resumed the form of a giant, abducted her and deposited her in a dungeon in his dingy stone castle. He also ate some of the apples, hoping it would keep him from growing older.

In the meantime, Odin and the other Aesir became concerned about Idunn's disappearance. Because she was not rejuvenating plants as usual, crops and forests across the world began to wither. Also, the gods worried that without Idunn's apples they would begin to age.

It was a relief, therefore, when the god Heimdall came forward and said he had seen Loki walking with Idunn on the day she vanished. That made Odin suspect Loki was involved, and when the All-Father pressed the trickster, he admitted what he had done. Odin ordered Loki to fix the situation immediately. Fearful of retribution by the other deities, Loki transformed himself into a hawk, flew to Thiazi's castle, and rescued the goddess. The giant gave chase. But as he approached Asgard, several Aesir intercepted and killed him.

Modern Portrayals of Loki

Arguably the most flamboyant and intriguing character in Norse mythology, Loki has been a natural subject of modern artistic and other cultural depictions. These have included paintings, sculptures, literature, operas, movies, and video games. The first major modern depictions of Loki came in the 1800s. Renowned German composer Richard Wagner included Loki in a series of operas based on the Norse and Germanic myths. Most often Wagner portrayed the trickster less as a villain and more as an ally of Odin and the other Aesir. In the more recent movies based on the Marvel comic book adaptations of the Norse myths, by contrast, Loki is plainly depicted as a villain. As played by actor Tom Hiddleston, he is both deceitful and undependable. Repeatedly, he causes trouble for and raises the ire of the god Thor (played as a stalwart hero by Chris Hemsworth). Loki also appears as the protagonist of Neil Gaiman's best-selling 2001 novel *American Gods*.

Loki and the Lethal Spear

Restored to her rightful place in Asgard, Idunn made sure that plants throughout the World Tree were back in their natural, healthy state. Loki hoped that this return to normalcy, coupled with his successful rescue of the goddess, would keep him in Odin's good graces. But although the All-Father did refrain from punishing the trickster, he warned him that he must not cause any further trouble or the consequences would be severe.

Unfortunately for all concerned, Loki wasted little time in committing the worst of all his offenses. Perhaps out of jealousy, he had always detested Baldur and how that god of purity was so widely loved and respected. So the trickster scowled as he watched Baldur's mother, Frigg, goddess of marriage, prepare for a ceremony intended to honor her son. She visited nearly every being and object in the world and got each to swear never to harm Baldur. That allowed the gods to play a game in which they hurled rocks and spears at him and watched them bounce off. (This happened because the rocks and the wood and metal in the spears had all promised Frigg they would not hurt her son.)

Hodur
The Norse god of darkness and winter who unwittingly killed Baldur, thanks to Loki

Furious over what he saw as a sickening display of hero worship, Loki went into action. He discovered that the only object in existence that had not promised never to hurt Baldur was mistletoe. So Loki stealthily attached some mistletoe to the tip of a spear, making that weapon potentially lethal to Baldur. The trickster then went to the meadow where the gods were tossing rocks and spears at the deity of purity. Noticing that Baldur's brother, Hodur, god of darkness, was not participating, Loki went to him and handed him the spear. According to Brian Branston, the smiling trickster said, "Here, pitch this shaft at him!"[18] Hodur did so, assuming the weapon would merely bounce off. Instead, it killed his brother in an instant.

Loki tricked Hodur into killing Baldur by attaching mistletoe to the end of a spear and guiding Hodur's arm as he threw it at Baldur, as shown in this picture.

Odin soon found out about Loki's role in Baldur's demise. This time Loki had gone too far. After chasing the trickster halfway around the World Tree, the gods caught up with him. They chained him in a dark, dismal cave, where they hoped he would remain, alone and incapacitated, for the rest of eternity. At that moment they could not foresee that the slippery trickster would eventually escape and do the worst damage yet to his fellow gods.

The Soul-Snatching Queen of Death

Initially, Hel did not like the area where Odin, leader of the Norse gods, had consigned her. Called Niflheim, it consisted of a series of gigantic underground caverns stretching thousands of miles. The area where Hel would soon reside was dubbed Helheim, meaning "Hidden." It was dimly lit, damp, and smelled of mold and ancient rot. But she would get used to it, the All-Father told her as they stood in the main meeting room of his palace.

Odin tried to put a positive spin on the situation. She was not being banished. Rather, she was being given the opportunity to rule over her own kingdom. Odin also intended to endow her with special powers that would allow her to run the place any way she wanted.

When Hel asked Odin what Helheim's purpose would be, he told her that it would be the largest of the World Tree's several death realms. Valhalla, which he himself presided over, housed the souls of heroic warriors who died in battle. And the sea goddess Ran oversaw a small domain reserved for those who had died by drowning. In comparison, Odin said, Helheim would be the largest final resting place for souls. It would house the spirits of humans and other beings who had died of old age, sickness, and accidents.

Niflheim
The World Tree's vast underworld, of which Hel's realm, Helheim, was a part

Finally, Hel asked the All-Father why he was doing this to her. Thinking it best to be honest with her, he admitted that he had no other choice. Years before, the trickster god Loki had mated with a giant named Angriboda, who had given birth to three monstrous children. First was the viscious wolf Fenrir; second was the slimy serpent Jormungander; and third was Hel herself. Odin reminded her that, by no fault of her own, one side of her body was that of a living woman, while the other side was that of a rotting corpse.

Angriboda
A giantess who mated with Loki and produced three monstrous offspring, including Hel

More importantly than her looks, however, the All-Father continued, an ancient prophecy had predicted that Loki's children would someday lead an evil army against the gods and humans. And to help keep that from happening, he must now confine those three beings to isolated places where their actions could be watched. In this way, says the thirteenth-century Norse document the *Prose Edda*, Hel ended up the ruler of Helheim. "She has a large residence there, and the walls are extremely high and the gate huge. Eljudner is the name of her hall, Hunger [is the name of] her [dinner] plate, Starving her knife, Ganglate her serving boy, Ganglot her serving woman."[19]

Creating a New Myth

Although Hel is consistently portrayed as one of the chief villains of Norse lore, she was not inherently evil, the way the Christian devil is typically portrayed. Nevertheless, as Daniel McCoy points out, she was "greedy, harsh, and cruel, or at least indifferent to the concerns of both the living and the dead."[20] These negative character traits are perhaps not surprising, some modern scholars suggest, considering her situation. She did not choose to rule the underworld but was instead forced into that role. And just as she normally refused to allow any of the souls she oversaw to leave, thanks to Odin she was trapped there herself.

Beyond the fact that Odin relegated Hel to the underworld and that she was a harsh ruler, little else is known about her. She appears in only one major myth. And none of the documents penned during the Viking age (from the late 700s to about 1000 CE)

This picture shows the children of Loki and the giant Angriboda: the serpent Jormungander, Hel (center), and the wolf Fenrir.

mention her at all. This and other evidence have led modern historians to suspect that Hel was not a character in the original pagan (non-Christian) Norse religion and myths. Instead, says respected Austrian scholar Rudolf Simek, she seems to have appeared after the Vikings converted to Christianity in the period from the late 900s to late 1000s. "On the whole," he states, "nothing speaks in favor of there being a belief in a goddess Hel in pre-Christian times."[21]

Indeed, the first known literary mention of Hel comes from the *Prose Edda*, penned by Icelandic writer Snorri Sturluson in the 1200s. Snorri deserves credit for preserving many Norse myths that would otherwise have been lost. However, the experts point out, he was an ardent Christian who wrote for a Christian audience. And evidently, he did not like that the original Norse tales lacked a devil-like character, an omission unacceptable to medieval Christians. Hence, it is possible that he created Hel and inserted her character into the existing collection of pagan tales, thereby creating a new myth.

Initial Feelings of Shock and Despair

Assuming that Snorri did add Hel's character to pagan Norse mythology, he could not have chosen a more dramatic and effective place to put her. She plays a major role in the pivotal myth in which Loki tricks Hodur, god of darkness, into killing Baldur, deity of light and purity. In the original pagan version, the story likely ended with the Aesir discovering that Loki was the real culprit and giving chase after he fled Asgard.

Snorri's version, in contrast, features an added section in which much attention is given to the fate of Baldur's soul. His spirit could not end up in Odin's realm of Valhalla, Snorri realized, because Baldur had not died in battle. And having his soul go to Helheim, where it would be trapped, would create plenty of dramatic tension. As told in the *Prose Edda*, therefore, upon Baldur's unexpected death, Hel snatched his spirit.

The reaction of the other gods to Baldur's death and the abduction of his soul was nothing less than heartrending. In Snorri's words, they "were struck speechless with horror." And at first

The Aesir React to Baldur's Death

In the *Prose Edda*, the thirteenth-century Icelandic writer Snorri Sturluson described the immediate reaction of Odin and the other gods to Baldur's sudden and unexpected death:

> The dart [spear] flew through him [Baldur], and he fell dead to the ground, and that was the greatest mishap ever caused among gods and men. After Baldur fell, the power of speech failed all the Aesir, as did the power of their hands to take him up [from the ground]. Each of them looked at the others and they were all of one mind towards the one who had done the deed. . . . When the Aesir tried to speak, the first thing to happen was that sobbing broke out, and none of them could express to each other their grief in words. But Odin took the loss the hardest, since he knew most clearly how great a damage and deprivation there was for the Aesir in Baldur's death.

Quoted in Andy Orchard, *Dictionary of Norse Myth and Legend*. London: Cassell, 1997, p. 12.

After Baldur died, his corpse was placed on his ship, which was burned while it drifted out into the open sea.

when they tried to discuss it, "the wailing so choked their voices that one could not describe to the other his sorrow."[22]

After they had managed to recover from their initial feelings of shock and despair, Odin, Frigg, and the other Aesir gave Baldur's lifeless body solemn funereal rites. They placed his corpse on his own ship, the *Hringhorni*. Then, following the custom of Viking funeral ceremonies accorded to well-to-do and powerful individuals, they burned the boat while it drifted out into the open sea.

Hermod's Long Journey

Following the funeral, the Aesir met to decide what could be done about recovering Baldur's soul. They knew that traditionally, Hel never released any of the spirits from her gloomy realm. But although she could be quite nasty and willful to deal with, Odin pointed out, she was not evil at heart. Perhaps she could be reasoned with in this instance. After all, Baldur had not been just another ordinary individual. Rather, he had been a widely beloved god and should therefore be considered a special case.

All the gods agreed that the mission to free Baldur's soul required the most diplomatic and well-spoken being they could find. Fortunately, such an individual existed within their own ranks. One

Hermod
The Aesir's trusted messenger god, who pleaded with Hel to release Baldur's soul

of Odin's many sons, he was the highly capable and trustworthy messenger god Hermod. For the vital task at hand, Odin fetched his own horse—Sleipnir, the world's fastest steed—and handed the reins to his son. After mounting the magnificent animal, Hermod reassured those present, promising to do everything he could to rescue their fellow deity. Then he galloped away at full speed.

Fleet-footed Sleipnir carried its earnest rider across multiple continents, passing through too many forests and mountain ranges to count. Finally, they reached the World Tree's enormous roots. There, according to Kevin Crossley-Holland, "for nine nights Hermod rode through a valley so deep and dark that he was unable to see anything. The ground fell away from him and the cold fingers of the underworld began to reach up towards him."[23] Finally, horse and rider reached the towering gate that marked the entrance to Hel's foreboding kingdom.

Baldur's Burning Funeral Ship

The late British scholar and mythologist Brian Branston colorfully described the traditional Viking funeral held by the Norse gods to honor the murdered Baldur:

> All kinds of people gathered for the burning. The mourners were led by Odin and Frigg. . . . Baldur's horse, in full harness, had already been put to death and laid on the pyre. And so the blazing funeral ship, with full sail set, left Asgard's shore. Darkness was falling and the great vessel began to gather way [speed] like a monstrous swan breasting the flame-flicked waves. . . . As the fire roared, the bulging sail glowed with the conflagration in front of it and those on shore saw the black rod of the mast . . . silhouetted before the amber light. Night came down. Soon the longship was raked from stem to stern with crackling fire until her planks were carbonized and her thicker ribs showed dark. Then in the far distance she was lost. Either what was left sank hissing into the sea, or else she dipped below the horizon and the spark winked out.

Brian Branston, *Gods and Heroes from Viking Mythology*. New York: Peter Bedrick, 1994, p. 137.

Hel's Bargain

After asking for and receiving an audience with Helheim's ruler, Hermod entered a large, musty-smelling chamber. Seeing the aged, disheveled queen perched on her wooden throne, he walked up to her and got right to the point. "He begged Queen Hel to let Baldur ride back home with him," Brian Branston wrote. "He explained how greatly the gods were grieving."[24]

At first, Hel seemed unmoved by his words and turned the rotten side of her face toward him. But as he continued to argue in highly moving terms, she appeared to soften somewhat and displayed the normal side of her face. As Branston put it, she told him, "It can soon be proved whether Baldur was as greatly loved as you say. Tell Frigg I will make a bargain with her. If every single creature up above, dead or alive, really is mourning for Baldur and is willing to shed tears to prove it, then he shall be restored to the gods. If but one single [being in the world] refuses to mourn, then Hel holds what she has."[25] When Hermod reported back to the Aesir, they all leaped into action. For days they asked beings from around the World Tree whether they had wept on hearing the news of Baldur's death. All said yes, with a single exception—a giantess named Thokk. Baldur had never done anything nice for her, she remarked. So there seemed no reason to weep for him.

As a result, Hel once again declined to let Baldur go. For that show of stubbornness, many Vikings saw the soul-snatching queen of Helheim as a villain. But others pointed out the story's twist ending. In time, the Aesir discovered to their horror, the giantess Thokk did not exist. "She" was actually the shape-shifting Loki in disguise. When it came to Norse mythical villains, therefore, Hel was no match for her father.

CHAPTER FOUR

The Trials and Deeds of Sigurd

At first glance, it may seem strange that one of the greatest human heroes in the collected Norse myths was a humble blacksmith and goldsmith. But according to the *Poetic Edda* and other surviving medieval documents, it was true. His name was Volund, and when he was not applying his widely renowned talents as a craftsman, he showed himself to be a fearless and expert warrior. He never asked for or started a fight, however. Only when forced into defending himself did he display his amazing combat skills.

That is exactly what occurred when a ruler who was unknown to Volund suddenly appeared at his forge. Nidud, king of a faraway Scandinavian realm, arrived with his queen and more than a dozen bodyguards. Without so much as a hello, the queen boldly demanded that Volund abandon his home and become the chief smith at Nidud's palace. Volund curtly refused. In response, Nidud ordered his guards to chain the smith and drag him away.

Nidud
The evil king who kidnapped Volund, one of the most popular of the Norse human heroes

When the group reached Nidud's kingdom, the guards deposited Volund on a small island near the capital city. There, he was told to begin making gold and silver jewelry and other decorative items for the royal family. The strong-willed and valiant craftsman had no intention of becoming their lackey, however. Employing one of his blacksmith tools, he severed his chain, slew the guard overseeing him, and swam from the island to the mainland.

Reaching the palace, Volund slipped through a servant's entrance. Entering a main corridor, he strangled the first sentry he encountered, took his sword and dagger, and found his way to the chambers where Nidud's two sons resided. Volund wasted no time in killing the princes, after which he stealthily carried the bodies to a workshop that adjoined the palace. There the intrepid smith proceeded to dismember the corpses. An excerpt from the *Poetic Edda* recounts how Volund "cut off the hands of those young cubs, and under the mud of the forge he laid their limbs. And their skulls . . . he [lined] in silver [and] gave to Nidud. And . . . their eyes he sent to Nidud's cunning wife."[26]

Having learned of the grisly deaths of their sons, the king and queen sent a squad of soldiers to kill Volund. But in an incredible display of fighting expertise, he swiftly dispatched them all. Then he returned to the workroom, swiftly fashioned a cape equipped with wings, and to the utter astonishment of onlookers, soared away into the sky.

Heroes with an Attitude

During the Viking age the legend of Volund was broadly popular throughout Scandinavia. He stood out among Norse mythology's cohort of memorable human heroes. Almost without exception, they were—like him—bold, courageous, and possessed of exceptional combat skills. Furthermore, also like Volund, they did not shy away from matching the brutality of their enemies with some considerable ferocity of their own.

Like real Viking warriors, the mythical human heroes did not fear death. This might have resulted in part from Viking religious beliefs. The Vikings believed that after their deaths, valiant warriors were destined to go to Valhalla. There they would mingle with the likes of Odin and become *einherjar*, members of his personal army of the dead.

Thus, real-life Viking fighters tended to strongly identify with mythical heroes like Volund. As a result, over time they developed an unusual view of death and the afterlife. "To put it bluntly,"

A Weird Sense of Humor Regarding Death

The Vikings developed a highly unusual view of what constituted both heroism and victory in warfare, says Saint Louis University scholar Tom Shippey. That included what today seems to be a weird tendency to joke and laugh when faced by impending death. "People who think like that," Shippey writes,

> can be beaten by a superior force, but though they can be killed like anyone else, they are impossible to daunt. If they're alive, they'll come back at you. They're not done until they're stone dead. Even if they're dying or helpless, they will try to think of some trick, and if you fall for it, then the joke's on you. . . . Humor is a vital part of the whole Viking mindset, as recorded in their own legends and in the legends and stories about them. . . . It goes along with the death cult. A hero is defined not by victory but by defeat. Only in defeat can you show that you will never give in. That's why the [Norse] gods have to die as well. If they did not die, how could they show true courage? If they were really immortal and invulnerable, who would respect them?

Tom Shippey, *Laughing Shall I Die: Lives and Deaths of the Great Vikings*. London: Reaktion, 2018, pp. 26, 37.

writes Saint Louis University scholar Tom Shippey, it was "a kind of death cult."[27] Its members, says Shippey, developed a kind of mental, emotional edge that inspired them to be fearless in battle. And accompanying this, he continues, was what now seems like a bizarre attitude toward both losing a fight and dying in it. In this unusual mindset, as Shippey explains,

> heroes may be outnumbered, betrayed, trapped, caught off-guard, or just plain run out of luck. That doesn't make you what we call a "loser." To their way of thinking, the only thing that would make you a loser would be giving up. And there's another factor, perhaps the most distinctive thing about the Viking mindset. . . . This was that the heroes of the Viking Age, both gods and men, fixated as they seemed to be on death and defeat, *just did not seem able to take death and defeat seriously*.[28]

Viking warriors were bold, fearless, and exceptional fighters, and most of Norse mythology's human heroes reflected these same characteristics.

Viking warriors valued courage far more than they feared death. In their world, a true warrior was more concerned with the fight than with the outcome—even to the point of making light of death. As Shippey writes, the Vikings believed it was best to show "you could turn the tables, spoil your enemy's victory, make a joke out of death, [and] die laughing."[29]

A Heritage of Bloodshed

Of the dozens of human heroes described in the Norse myths, all of whom possessed the unique mindset Shippey describes, Sigurd was among the most celebrated. He was the grandson of Volsung, a noted warrior whose name was attached to a family line of heroic fighters—the Volsungs. It was said that Volsung himself was a direct descendant of Odin, so all of the Volsungs, including Sigurd, supposedly possessed divine blood.

Volsung
A warrior who was the namesake of a renowned family line of Norse human heroes

Sigurd's journey to hero status followed the exploits of both his grandfather and father. The most well-known myth involving Sigurd's father—the hero Sigmund—places him at a wedding celebration when a one-eyed man mysteriously appears, draws a magnificent sword, and plunges it into the trunk of a large tree. Whoever could draw the sword from the tree, the man declared, would be destined for great things. After the stranger disappeared into thin air, everyone present suspected that it had been Odin himself.

No one was able to pull the sword free until Sigmund stepped forward and did it easily. Then, in an unexpected twist, out of jealousy and a desire to possess the weapon himself, the local king slew Sigmund's father, the hero Volsung. The king also brutally executed all of Volsung's sons, except Sigmund. After escaping the slaughter, Sigmund plotted revenge and eventually killed the murderous king with the very sword that ruler coveted so much.

Two Widely Popular Dragons

Over the years literary experts and ordinary readers alike have noticed marked similarities between two widely popular dragons from literature. One is the Norse dragon Fafnir. The other is Smaug, the dragon in *The Hobbit* by English writer J.R.R. Tolkien. Their similarity is no accident. For his own writings, Tolkien borrowed freely from the themes, situations, and characters of the Norse and Germanic myths. For instance, both Fafnir and Smaug guard stolen treasures. Also, because Fafnir started life as a human being, he retains the ability to speak even after he turns into a dragon. Likewise, as scholar Carolyne Larrington points out, "Smaug can talk. He has a long conversation with Bilbo the hobbit, who distracts him with [riddles] while he spies out the dragon's vulnerable spot." Another similarity is that both the Norse myth about Fafnir and the incidents involving Smaug in Tolkien's work explore the theme of the destructive power of greed.

Carolyne Larrington, *The Norse Myths: A Guide to the Gods and Heroes*. London: Thames and Hudson, 2017, p. 141.

Shortly after these events transpired, Sigmund, who was now king, married, and soon his wife gave birth to Sigurd. As the late Scottish mythologist Donald A. Mackenzie described the child, "Bright were his eyes, and his face was kingly. . . . He grew up to be strong and fearless; a warrior's skill had he and Volsung pride, and he had great wisdom, and was eloquent of speech. . . . The lad grew to manhood's strength and wisdom while he was yet young."[30]

So impressive was Sigurd that his maternal uncle, Gripir, predicted the young man would achieve both fame and greatness. "You will be of men the mightiest under the sun," Gripir told him, "the highest born of any prince."[31]

A Life of Adventure

Gripir's words proved prophetic, as Sigurd went on to have a life filled with adventure, dangerous trials, and valiant deeds. One of his most famous accomplishments is told in a tale that begins with his father, Sigmund. A warrior named Lyngvi had quarreled with Sigmund, and so the two met on the battlefield to settle the issue. There, the sword Sigmund had years before pulled from the tree shattered. Seeing this opening, Lyngvi leaped upon Sigmund and killed him.

Regin
In the story of Sigurd's adventures, his foster father and tutor

It then fell to Sigurd to avenge his father's death. Before setting out to do this, Sigurd asked his foster father, a skilled blacksmith named Regin, to rebuild Sigmund's shattered sword. The result was a formidable weapon that Sigurd called Gram. Next the young hero challenged Lyngvi, who raised a small army for the fight. In that battle, as told in the Icelandic *Volsunga Saga*, "Sigurd went forward past the banners with the sword Gram in his hand. He cut both men and horses and went through the ranks, so that both of his arms were covered in blood to the shoulder. Men fled before him as he went, and neither helmet nor mail-coat could withstand him. No one thought that they had ever seen his like before."[32] Eventually, Sigurd reaches Lyngvi and, using Gram, cuts him to pieces.

One of Sigurd's most celebrated achievements was the slaying of an enormous dragon, which he did by plunging his sword, Gram, up to the hilt into the beast.

Earning the Nickname Dragonslayer

In spite of the glory heaped on Sigurd for that display of fighting prowess, his most renowned achievement was slaying an enormous dragon. The young man was in his twenties when Regin suggested that he track down and slay the creature, called Fafnir. Fafnir had originally been a man who had stolen a huge treasure of coins and precious jewels. Unknown to the thief, however, within that trove was a ring infused with a magic spell, a curse that caused him to be transformed into a monstrous dragon. Fafnir now dwelled in a remote cave, Regin said, where he jealously guarded the treasure.

Sigurd accepted the challenge, and accompanied by Regin, he traveled to the cave. Once there, Sigurd dug several ditches in front of the cave entrance and crouched down in one of them. His strategy was to stab the beast as it walked overhead. That plan worked. A few hours later, Mackenzie wrote, "Fafnir crawled from his lair, roaring and spouting venom . . . [and Sigurd] plunged his sword Gram through the dragon right up to the hilt."[33]

Afterward, as the two men stood beside the huge carcass, Regin tried to share credit by pointing out that he had forged the sword that had pierced the monster's heart. But Sigurd saw it differently. As if confirming the Norse warrior's belief that having raw courage ensured victory no matter what, he remarked, "Better in battle is a brave heart than a strong sword."[34]

Ragnar's Revenge

The Icelandic Viking Egil Skallagrimsson, whose long life spanned most of the 900s CE, was the type of man that most people knew they should not cross. He was a farmer, but he was also sometimes a warrior who joined raiding parties that plundered villages on distant shores. Egil also had a nasty temper. When he felt someone had wronged him, he set his sights on revenge. It was said that he had begun his habit of seeking retribution at the tender age of seven. When one of his playmates cheated him in a game, young Egil got hold of an ax and cleaved the other boy's head in two. According to the Icelandic story *Egil's Saga*, in the years and decades that followed, a number of other individuals who angered Egil paid for it with their lives.

Bodvar
Warrior-poet Egil Skallagrimsson's son, who died in a drowning accident

Yet there was a part of Egil's personality that stood squarely in opposition to his temper and the violence it triggered. He was as skilled with words as he was with weapons. And he left behind a number of poignant poems that have survived to the present. Particularly touching is *Sonatorrek*, which he penned after his son, Bodvar, accidentally drowned. "My tongue's a deadweight, dumb as iron," Egil wrote in one verse. He added that it was impossible to express how deeply sad he was. The right words were simply "too heavy to drag from the mind's dark[ness]."[35] Many generations of readers have pointed out how the beauty of the work belies the poet's perception that he had little to say that was meaningful.

Later in life, however, Egil was less thoughtful and frequently lost his temper. Matters came to a head when a kinsman of Viking king Eric Bloodaxe's wife, Queen Gunnhilder, publicly insulted Egil. In response, Egil killed the man. Next, in retaliation, the royal couple declared Egil an outlaw. Egil struck back by slaying Eric's and Gunnhilder's son, Rognvalder.

Eventually, Egil was captured and sentenced by King Eric to die the next morning. However, overnight the prisoner composed a long poem that praised the king. And when Eric heard it recited the next day, he was so impressed that he granted Egil his life. The burly, temperamental poet-warrior ended up returning to his farm in Iceland, where he lived well into his eighties.

Viking Customs Surrounding Revenge

Although Egil's life was definitely more eventful and colorful than those of most Vikings, his penchant for obtaining revenge when slighted was far from unusual. Such attempts to seek retribution were fairly common in Scandinavia during the Viking age. One important reason was that as a rule, there were no written laws someone could have recourse to if they felt their honor had been challenged. So it was expected that a person who felt that way would resort to violence, especially in the form of vengeance.

This was particularly the case when the person who had been slighted or insulted was widely perceived as a hero. Heroic individuals—especially heroic warriors—were so revered in Norse society that most people approved of their attempts to get justice, even when it took the form of revenge. That was certainly the case with Egil. The courage, defiance, and resistance he displayed after being condemned as an outlaw made him a folk hero. And most Vikings were hugely relieved when King Eric spared his life.

The customs surrounding the seeking of justice in this manner—for heroes and nonheroes alike—were deeply imbedded in Norse society. In some Viking areas, disputes over land ownership, who was a rightful ruler, and so forth, could be resolved by prominent members of the community. The arguing parties brought their grievances before a group of older men widely seen to be wise and just. At times the two parties accepted the

Viking ruler Eric Bloodaxe is shown here claiming his bride. After Egil killed one of Eric's wife's kinsmen, he was sentenced to death by the king.

settlement suggested by those elders. Fairly often it consisted of one party paying the other money, farm animals, or something else of value as compensation. But when no settlement could be reached, the dispute could escalate into a long-running feud that could last for years and in some cases even generations.

When personal honor was involved, and especially when the injured party was seen as a heroic warrior, such disputes often led to revenge killings. Today they would be seen as murder, plain and simple. In Viking society, however, free men and women—particularly admired warriors—had an unwritten right to carry out such killings. "You could kill somebody in public without suffering serious consequences," say the researchers at the online Ancient Origins website. This could be done as long as "you were honest and did not hide your actions and gave others [in the community] the opportunity to react. It was important to take responsibility for the murder and not run away."[36] The killer, or his or her family, usually had to pay the victim's family monetary compensation. As long as this was done, the matter was seen as settled. Thus, in a very real sense, as Ingrid P. Nuse, an expert on Norwegian history and culture, quips, "You could get away with killing someone, but only as long as you were honest about it."[37]

A Hero of Epic Proportions

These customs surrounding the issues of honor, feuds, and revenge killings pertained mainly to the members of Norse society.

Not Destined to Meet Odin

Egil Skallagrimsson's poem *Sonatorrek*, written in memory of his son who had recently drowned, dates from roughly 1230 CE. In the two stanzas selected here, Egil laments his son's demise. Then he alludes to the reality that, because the son did not die in battle, the young man has no chance of becoming a heroic warrior. And that means he will not end up in Odin's paradise for such heroes—Valhalla. This shows how important attaining heroic status was among Norse warriors. (The "shield-tree" he mentions is the linden tree, from which the Vikings made most of their shields. If only there had been time for his son to train as a soldier, Egil seems to say, using the tree as a metaphor, the boy might have become one of Odin's heroic followers in heaven.)

The sea's grievously
seized much from me,
it's grim to recall
my son's fall
after the shield
of my family
sank lifeless
on the way to joy.

I know in myself
my son would never
have warped
into a wicked warrior—
if that shield-tree
were allowed to ripen
until he took up
arms for Odin.

Quoted in Andrew Smardon, "Ideas of North: Egill Skallagrimsson's *Sonatorrek*," Ideas of North. www.ideasofnorth.com.

Two Vikings, with spectators looking on, fight. In Viking society, disputes often led to revenge killings.

It was a very different story when a foreigner killed a prominent Viking. In such cases members of his family, or any concerned Vikings for that matter, felt justified or even compelled to strike back with impunity. No compensation was deemed necessary, and there was no limit to the scope and brutality of the retribution.

Perhaps the most famous example of this sort of vengeance was that surrounding the demise of a Viking hero of truly epic proportions. His name was Ragnar Lothbrok, and he supposedly flourished in the 800s CE, though it is still not certain whether he was a real person. According to Utrecht University professor Emma Groeneveld, it is entirely possible that

> in the centuries after the adventurous 9th-century Viking heyday of raids, stories cropped up to unify various historical events and known persons under one roof. Several historians have indeed argued that Ragnar Lothbrok may be an amalgam [blend] of various historical figures, tied together into one mythical hero who was the scourge [punisher] of 9th-century CE northern Europe.[38]

Whether or not Ragnar actually existed, Viking society from about 900 CE on was absolutely convinced he had been a real person. And each new generation grew up retelling, and often embellishing, the tales of his exploits. Moreover, the perception among the Norse was that he was treated badly by a foreign king. The king's monstrous behavior toward a revered Viking ensured that his fellow Vikings would clamor for revenge.

Gaining Widespread Fame Overnight

The first few of Ragnar's purported exploits were said to have occurred when he was quite young—likely in his early twenties. Already a highly skilled warrior, he was the son of Denmark's King Sigurd Ring. Ragnar's skill was evident on many occasions, including one in which he killed a bear and a vicious wild dog that had attacked him simultaneously.

King Sigurd Ring
Ragnar Lothbrok's legendary father, from whom Ragnar inherited the Danish kingship

Not long afterward, it was said, Ragnar followed up that feat by killing a dragon. Word had spread that the pet snake of a Swedish princess named Thora had inexplicably grown into a huge, terrifying reptile. And Ragnar reasoned that if he could dispatch the beast he would gain widespread fame overnight. So he traveled to Sweden and confronted the creature. A surviving medieval chronicle describing Ragnar's life claims that the young man fearlessly assaulted the monster and "pierced its heart with his spear. Then he drew his sword and cut off the serpent's head."[39]

It was also during his young adulthood that Ragnar met and wed his three wives. The first was a shield-maiden (woman warrior) named Lagertha. After divorcing her, he married the Swedish princess Thora. And when she died shortly afterward of an unknown illness, he wed a Norwegian farm girl named Aslaug. With these women Ragnar sired at least nine children, including his

Ragnar's Death Song

The story of Ragnar Lothbrok's defiance in the face of death added one last, valiant flourish to his image as an epic hero. But this story came long after his death. In the 1100s, almost three centuries after Ragnar's execution by a foreign king, an anonymous Viking poet wrote down the words Ragnar was said to have uttered in his last moments of life. These words appear in a poem titled *Krakumal*, often called the "Death Song of Ragnar Lothbrok."

In one stanza, Ragnar says that "the benches of Baldur's father [are] prepared for feasting." Baldur's father is the god Odin. And the "benches" are in the dining hall in Odin's realm of dead heroes—Valhalla, where Ragnar is certain he will soon go. In another stanza, Ragnar foresees that his sons will seek revenge for his death, saying that their "hearts are strong" and that they "will swell with anger for their father to be avenged." Ragnar predicts that the gods will invite him into their kingdom of Asgard. And finally, he heroically thumbs his nose at his executioners by using humor to show he is unafraid of death. "Laughing shall I die," he tells them.

Quoted in Tom Shippey, *Laughing Shall I Die: Lives and Deaths of the Great Vikings*. London: Reaktion, 2018, p. 87.

later famous sons Ivar the Boneless, Bjorn Ironside, and Sigurd Snake-in-the-Eye.

Facing Death with a Smile

In the meantime, Ragnar's father passed away and left him the Danish throne. With his newfound political and military power, he invaded several neighboring regions. And in the course of a few years, the tales about him claim, he managed to seize control of sizable sections of Norway and Sweden. Often, he fought right alongside his men, in the thick of the fray, and was wounded many times. Thanks to these exploits, as well as to the land and riches many of his followers gained, his reputation as a true hero swiftly grew.

For his next adventure, Ragnar went after some of the small kingdoms that then made up England. So confident was he of success that he boasted he could take over all of England with

Ragnar Lothbrok leads a raid into Britain. Viking society often told and retold tales of his exploits.

only enough soldiers to fill two ships. This display of overconfidence did not serve Ragnar well. When he invaded the kingdom of Northumbria in northern England, the local king, Aella, raised a large army and "marched against Ragnar with an overwhelming host," according to the medieval chronicle *The Tale of Ragnar's Sons*. In the massive battle, "almost all [of Ragnar's] men were killed, but he himself charged four times through the ranks [toward] King Aella."[40] Royal bodyguards were able to protect Aella, however, and they eventually captured the exhausted Ragnar.

Aella
The ruler of the English kingdom of Northumbria, who captured and executed Ragnar

Aella wanted to make an example of Ragnar. The Northumbrian ruler hoped this would dissuade other Vikings from attacking northern England. To that purpose, Aella had his soldiers toss Ragnar into a pit containing dozens of poisonous snakes. The king and his henchmen were totally unprepared for what happened next, however. Instead of showing fear and begging for his life, Ragnar proceeded to demonstrate the unique and defiant attitude of Viking warriors facing imminent death. Supposedly, he smiled broadly and casually said, "The hours of life have passed, and laughing shall I die."[41]

Although Ragnar was unable to achieve revenge himself, he received it in a big way posthumously through the efforts of his sons. Led by Ivar the Boneless, they raised an army, invaded Northumbria, and scored an overwhelming victory. As for Aella, *The Tale of Ragnar's Sons* tells how "the greater part of his forces fell, [and] he himself was taken captive. Ivar and the brothers now recall[ed] how their father was tortured."[42] To avenge Ragnar, his sons responded in kind by torturing and executing the man that they and all Vikings saw as a villain of the first order. The Northumbrian king had learned the hard way how serious Viking warriors were about achieving vengeance on someone who had dared to wrong a revered Norse hero.

Loyalty and Valor: Norse Heroines

In a past age now lost in the mists of time, the young, stalwart hero Helgi Hundingsbane led his soldiers to a place called Logafell, where an enemy force was waiting. Soon "the warriors forth to the battle went,"[43] according to *The First Lay of Helgi*, part of the larger *Poetic Edda*. In the hours that followed, Helgi and his men attained a clear victory, although many died on both sides.

As the victor knelt on the battlefield, trying to rest his weary limbs, a blindingly bright light suddenly shown from above. "From that light," *The First Lay of Helgi* recounts, "flashes [of lightning] leaped." Helgi looked upward and beheld a swarm of Valkyries descending, each female warrior riding a powerful steed whose hide glowed with a mysterious light. "And from their spears the sparks flew forth."[44]

Helgi watched as the warrior women searched through the piles of bodies. Clearly, they were looking for chosen fighters, whose bodies they would bear to faraway Valhalla to live with the divine Odin. Helgi himself, he realized, had not yet been so selected because he had survived the battle. Only dead heroes were eligible for the honor of dwelling with the gods.

And yet, to the exhausted, blood-spattered man's surprise, he saw that one of the magnificent-looking women was approaching him. She told him her name was Sigrun. She had long admired him from afar, she said, and now she badly needed his help. At first, Helgi was awestruck that he was actually conversing with one of Odin's legendary female servants. But that feeling swiftly faded. Her lilting voice and spectacular beauty enthralled him, and he could feel himself rapidly falling in love with her.

Sigrun
A Valkyrie who fell in love with the noted hero Helgi Hundingsbane

When Helgi asked the armor-laden maiden why she had need of him, she explained that her father, King Hogni, had betrothed her to a warrior named Hothbrodd. But she viewed Hothbrodd as an uncouth lout who was not worthy of her. She implored Helgi to help her keep what would undoubtedly be an unhappy marriage from coming to pass.

Thereafter, events proceeded with amazing speed. Only a few hours after their initial meeting, Helgi and Sigrun concluded they were soulmates, and he pledged to aid her in her plight. After raising another army, he defeated and killed Hogni and slew Hothbrodd as well. Not long after that, Helgi and Sigrun wed, and in the years that followed, they had several children together.

Female Warriors: Real or Strictly Mythical?

The Valkyries, supernatural female warriors, played frequent and important roles in a number of famous Norse myths. In the artistic renderings produced during and after the Viking age, they were most often shown riding flying horses that hovered high above battlefields. When the time was right, the Valkyries glided downward and scooped up chosen heroic fighters who had been killed in combat and took them to Odin's death realm of Valhalla. Hence, the meaning of the term *Valkyries* in the old Norse language is "choosers of the slain."

H.R.E. Davidson offered more detail about these singular beings. Sometimes, she said, writers and artists depicted them as having "giant stature, striding across the mountains or appearing in time of danger to take up the hero and to carry him out of his predicament. They are said . . . to vary their appearance and to be seen sometimes as fearsome beings and sometimes as beautiful maidens who offer love to the warrior."[45]

The mystical Valkyries are not the only female warriors who appear in the Norse myths. There are also some so-called

This picture shows a Valkyrie with a dying hero. The Valkyries scooped up chosen heroic fighters who had been killed in combat and took them to Valhalla.

shield-maidens, human female fighters said to have fought in battles. One question that historians still debate is where the image of these mythical shield-maidens came from. Were they based on, and simply a human version of, the Valkyries? Or were the latter inspired by real Viking women who sometimes fought in battle beside the men?

No firm consensus among scholars on this topic has yet been reached. However, a fairly recent development suggests that at least a few Viking shield-maidens did exist. In the 1870s excavators unearthed a grave in the Swedish town of Birka. It held a human skeleton surrounded by a large array of weaponry, including a sword, dagger, battle-ax, spear, and two shields. For many decades experts assumed the skeleton belonged to a male Viking fighter. But in 2017 DNA analysis conclusively proved that the grave belonged to a woman. Based on this evidence, some historians suggest that the mythical Valkyries and shield-maidens may have inspired a small number of Norse women to take up arms. And the individual buried in Birka was one of those women.

Love at First Sight

Whether or not shield-maidens were real, a fair number of them did inhabit the Norse myths, along with their fellow female fighters, the Valkyries. Like Sigrun, several of the Valkyries had their own myths. Of those, arguably the best known today is that of Brunhilda. Several versions of her tale have survived, and in the Icelandic one she is described as Odin's daughter. When one day she challenged his authority, the story goes, he put her into a deep sleep, deposited her on a desolate mountaintop, and created a lofty wall of flames around that peak.

Brunhilda
One of the Valkyries, she was rescued from a perpetual deep sleep by the hero Sigurd

An unknown span of time elapsed, and the beautiful Valkyrie remained comatose and cut off from the rest of the world. She had no way of knowing about the mission of the human hero Sigurd to slay the treasure-guarding dragon Fafnir. By chance, the place where the young man fought the beast was situated only a few miles from the mountaintop where Brunhilda lay. After dispatching the dragon, Sigurd heard a rumor that a fair maiden

The Valkyries' Ride Set to Music

Over the centuries the Norse myths about the Valkyries have inspired a good deal of art, including paintings, sculptures, and musical works. The single most famous piece of music depicting those supernatural warrior women is German composer Richard Wagner's *Ride of the Valkyries*, completed in 1856. Part of his opera *The Valkyrie*, it provides an exciting backdrop for a scene in which eight Valkyries prepare to fly to a battlefield and retrieve the souls of heroes who have died in the fighting. From the early twentieth century to the present, music lovers have not needed to attend performances of *The Valkyrie* in order to hear this music. It is so melodic and exciting that numerous movies and TV shows have used it as part of their musical scores. Among others, these movies include D.W. Griffith's epic 1915 film *Birth of a Nation*, Francis Ford Coppola's *Apocalypse Now* (1979), the *Blues Brothers* (1980), and *Rango* (2011). On TV the *Ride of the Valkyries* appeared in the popular 1960s show *Lost in Space*, and more recently *For All Mankind* (2021).

needed rescuing from a nearby mountain peak, and his stalwart horse, Grani, carried him there at top speed.

Reaching the wall of fire, the young hero was undaunted. According to the late mythologist Brian Branston's account of the story, he shouted to his steed, "On, Grani, on! Leap this blazing barrier! Only you can do it!"[46] In an astounding feat of strength, Grani soared upward and carried his rider over the flames and into a courtyard. There, on a wide marble pedestal, Brunhilda lay unmoving. At that moment, a small sparrow descended to the pedestal and chirped at Sigurd, who was blessed with the ability to decipher the language of birds. To awaken the sleeping maiden, the sparrow said, the man need only kiss her lightly on the forehead. Sigurd did so, and a few seconds later Brunhilda opened her eyes.

The young woman sat up and gazed at her rescuer. And in that instant something seemingly miraculous occurred. As the two locked eyes, they fell completely and hopelessly in love. "I

Viking warriors feast in Valhalla after being taken there by the Valkyries.

swear by Odin's wrath," she said (according to Branston), "that I will never love any man but you." Sigurd replied, "I swear by my sword, Gram, the gift of Odin himself, that my love for you will never die."[47]

In the years that followed, Brunhilda and Sigurd's mutual love never wavered. Yet their relationship did take some unexpected and unfortunate twists and turns. An evil person gave Sigurd a magic potion that made him forget all about Brunhilda. Not knowing about that drink, in a fit of anger she had him killed. Still in love with him, however, she was overcome with guilt and regret. In a display that made onlookers gasp, she threw herself into the flames of his funeral pyre. Her last words were, "Together we will rise to Odin in Valhalla!"[48] Soon afterward, the groom of Sigurd's horse Grani reported that he witnessed the stallion flying off into the sky, bearing a man and woman on his back.

A Fabled and Admired Figure

Another warrior woman in the Norse myths fell in love with a male hero. And like Brunhilda, she later became momentarily furious with him. In this case the woman was the legendary shieldmaiden Lagertha, and the male hero was the adventuresome Ragnar Lothbrok.

Lagertha
The legendary Norwegian shieldmaiden who married the hero Ragnar Lothbrok

Since both Lagertha and Ragnar were skilled fighters, it is not surprising that they met in a military setting. This came about not long after a Norwegian king, Siward, who was Ragnar's grandfather, was killed by an enemy—Sweden's King Fro.

Ragnar, who had recently inherited Denmark's throne from his father, was outraged by Siward's murder and swore to wreak vengeance on Fro. To that end, Ragnar went to Norway and began raising an army. There, several women approached him, and it impressed him that they were dressed like male warriors and wielded swords and shields. When they offered

Portrayals of Lagertha over the Centuries

The first known literary depiction of the legendary Viking shield-maiden Lagertha was the *Gesta Danorum*, a chronicle penned in the 1100s by the Danish historian Saxo Grammaticus. He assumed she was a real person and presented her myth as if it were a historical work. She was also mentioned in the thirteenth-century Icelandic sagas. Artistic presentations of Lagertha began in 1789 with the play *Lagertha* by Norwegian playwright Christen Pram. Then came an 1801 ballet based on her story, staged by noted Italian-born Danish ballet master Vincenzo Galeotti. Lagertha's character later appeared in various novels and literary works. But by far the most popular and colorful version of her exploits was the TV miniseries *Vikings*. Airing from 2013 to 2020, that spectacular and well-reviewed Canadian-Irish production focused on the adventures of the Norse hero Ragnar Lothbrok and his wives and sons. Lagertha was portrayed, to widespread critical acclaim, by Canadian actress Katheryn Winnick.

to fight for him, he welcomed them to his forces, and in the battle that ensued, which Ragnar won, the women fought bravely.

Ragnar was particularly impressed by one of these shield-maidens, named Lagertha. In fact, he learned that she had killed so many enemy soldiers that she had turned the tide of battle in his favor. The impulsive Ragnar wasted little time in proposing marriage to her, and she accepted. They were happy together for three years, but then he returned to Denmark and fell for the Swedish princess Thora. After Ragnar divorced Lagertha, she was naturally angry and hurt, but she remained steadfastly loyal to him as an ally in war. When he later needed reinforcements to fend off an enemy army, she came to his rescue with more than one hundred ships filled with fighters.

Thus, Lagertha became a fabled and admired figure among later generations of Vikings. Her faithfulness to the flawed but extraordinary Ragnar, coupled with her military skills and valor, made her a true heroine.

Furthermore, these mythical heroines, along with any real Norse shield-maidens that may have existed, testify to another unusual trait of Viking culture. Most other ancient and medieval societies viewed women as decidedly inferior to men. In contrast, says historian Joshua J. Mark, Norse culture seems to have valued women enough to "attribute to them the same martial [fighting] skills and ability to determine their own fate as men were allowed."[49] Despite their warlike tendencies and other faults, it seems the Vikings were in at least one way far ahead of their time.

SOURCE NOTES

Introduction: Courage in the Face of Suffering

1. Robert Cook, trans., *The Complete Sagas of Icelanders*. Reykjavik: Leifur Eiriksson, 1997, p. 93.
2. H.R.E. Davidson, *Gods and Myths of Northern Europe*. Baltimore, MD: Penguin, 1972, p. 218.
3. Edith Hamilton, *Mythology*. New York: Grand Central, 1999, p. 301.
4. Hamilton, *Mythology*, p. 306.

Chapter One: Thor Versus the Giants

5. Quoted in Kevin Crossley-Holland, *Norse Myths: Tales of Odin, Thor, and Loki*. Somerville, MA: Candlewick Studio, 2017, p. 144.
6. Crossley-Holland, *Norse Myths: Tales of Odin, Thor, and Loki*, p. 148.
7. Davidson, *Gods and Myths of Northern Europe*, p. 84.
8. Hamilton W. Mabie, *Norse Mythology: Great Stories from the Eddas*. Mineola, NY: Dover, 2015, p. 30.
9. Quoted in Neil Gaiman, *Norse Mythology*. New York: Norton, 2017, p. 120.
10. Gaiman, *Norse Mythology*, p. 123.

Chapter Two: Troubles with Two-Faced Loki

11. Quoted in Brian Branston, *Gods and Heroes from Viking Mythology*. New York: Peter Bedrick, 1994, p. 60.
12. Branston, *Gods and Heroes from Viking Mythology*, p. 64.
13. Davidson, *Gods and Myths of Northern Europe*, p. 176.
14. Hamilton, *Mythology*, p. 310.
15. John Lindow, *Handbook of Norse Mythology*. Oxford, UK: ABC-CLIO, 2001, p. 219.
16. Daniel McCoy, *The Viking Spirit: An Introduction to Norse Mythology and Religion*. Self-published, CreateSpace Independent Publishing Platform, 2016, p. 181.
17. Crossley-Holland, *Norse Myths: Tales of Odin, Thor, and Loki*, p. 65.
18. Quoted in Branston, *Gods and Heroes from Viking Mythology*, p. 136.

Chapter Three: The Soul-Snatching Queen of Death

19. Quoted in Lindow, *Handbook of Norse Mythology*, p. 172.
20. Daniel McCoy, "Hel," Norse Mythology for Smart People. https://norse-mythology.org.
21. Rudolph Simek, *Dictionary of Northern Mythology*, trans. Angela Hall. Rochester, NY: Boydell and Brewer, 1996, p. 138.
22. Snorri Sturluson, *The Prose Edda*, trans. R.B. Anderson. Madison: University of Wisconsin, 1879, p. 44.
23. Kevin Crossley-Holland, *The Norse Myths*. New York: Pantheon, 1980, p. 158.
24. Branston, *Gods and Heroes from Viking Mythology*, p. 140.
25. Quoted in Branston, *Gods and Heroes from Viking Mythology*, p. 140.

Chapter Four: The Trials and Deeds of Sigurd

26. Quoted in Carolyne Larrington, *The Norse Myths: A Guide to the Gods and Heroes*. London: Thames and Hudson, 2017, p. 76.
27. Tom Shippey, *Laughing Shall I Die: Lives and Deaths of the Great Vikings*. London: Reaktion, 2018, p. 14.
28. Shippey, *Laughing Shall I Die*, p. 26.
29. Shippey, *Laughing Shall I Die*, p. 26.
30. Donald A. Mackenzie, *Teutonic Myth and Legend*. London: Gresham, 1912, p. 314.
31. Quoted in Andy Orchard, *Dictionary of Norse Myth and Legend*. London: Cassell, 1997, p. 144.
32. Quoted in Orchard, *Dictionary of Norse Myth and Legend*, p. 107.
33. Quoted in Mackenzie, *Teutonic Myth and Legend*, p. 317.
34. Quoted in Mackenzie, *Teutonic Myth and Legend*, p. 318.

Chapter Five: Ragnar's Revenge

35. Quoted in Andrew Smardon, "Ideas of North: Egill Skallagrimsson's *Sonatorrek*," Ideas of North. www.ideasofnorth.com.
36. Ancient Origins, "Never Offend a Viking or 'the Thing' Might Just Decide Your Fate," December 1, 2017. www.ancient-origins.net.
37. Ingrid P. Nuse, "How Vikings Could Get Away with Murder." RealClearScience. www.realclearscience.com.

38. Emma Groeneveld, "Ragnar Lothbrok," World History Encyclopedia, August 31, 2018. www.worldhistory.org.
39. Quoted in Northvegr Foundation, "The Tale of Ragnar's Sons: Part 1," trans. Peter Tunstall, January 1, 2005. https://jillian.rootaction.net.
40. Quoted in Northvegr Foundation, "The Tale of Ragnar's Sons: Part 2," trans. Peter Tunstall, January 1, 2005. https://jillian.rootaction.net.
41. Quoted in Shippey, *Laughing Shall I Die*, p. 87.
42. Northvegr Foundation, "The Tale of Ragnar's Sons: Part 2."

Chapter Six: Loyalty and Valor: Norse Heroines

43. Henry A. Bellows, trans., *The Poetic Edda*. Princeton, NJ: Princeton University Press, 1936, p. 294.
44. Bellows, *The Poetic Edda*, p. 295.
45. H.R.E. Davidson, *Scandinavian Mythology*. London: Paul Hamlyn, 1969, p. 41.
46. Quoted in Branston, *Gods and Heroes from Viking Mythology*, p. 86.
47. Quoted in Branston, *Gods and Heroes from Viking Mythology*, p. 86.
48. Quoted in Branston, *Gods and Heroes from Viking Mythology*, p. 88.
49. Joshua J. Mark, "Ten Legendary Female Viking Warriors," World History Encyclopeida, January 9, 2019. www.worldhistory.org.

FOR FURTHER RESEARCH

Books

Padraic Colum, *Loki: The Mischief Behind the Legend*. Monument, CO: Wordfire, 2022.

Jason Dodd, *Norse Mythology: A Collection of the Best Norse Myths*. West Sacramento, CA: Rivercat, 2024.

Dorling Kindersley, *Eyewitness: Viking*. New York: Dorling Kindersley, 2024.

Gunnar Hylnsson, *Norse Myths, Paganism, Magic, Vikings, and Runes*. Self-published, 2022.

Carolyne Larrington, *The Norse Myths That Shape the Way We Think*. London: Thames and Hudson, 2023.

Mathias Nordwig, *Norse Mythology for Kids*. Eagle, ID: Rockridge, 2020.

Henry Romano, *Myths and Legends of the Norse*. London: DTTY, 2022.

Internet Sources

Thomas Apel, "Loki," Mythopedia, December 8, 2022. https://mythopedia.com.

Thomas Apel, "Tyr," Mythopedia, March 8, 2023. https://mythopedia.com.

Lara Colrain, "Norse Pantheon: 10 Fascinating Gods and Goddesses," The Collector, October 21, 2023. www.thecollector.com.

Emma Groeneveld, "Bjorn Ironside," World History Encyclopedia, December 4, 2018. www.worldhistory.org.

Emma Groeneveld, "Ragnar Lothbrok," World History Encyclopedia, August 31, 2018. www.worldhistory.org.

Joshua J. Mark, "Ten Norse Mythology Facts You Need to Know," World History Encyclopedia, September 21, 2021. www.worldhistory.org.

Robbie Mitchell, "Jotunheim: Outsized Tales from the Norse Land of the Giants," Ancient Origins, September 25, 2022. www.ancient-origins.net.

Odin's Treasures, "Ragnar Lothbrok: Separating the Man from the Myth," 2024. https://odinstreasures.com.

Sons of the Vikings, "Viking Lore: A Quick Intro to Norse Eddas and Sagas," July 3, 2020. https://sonsofvikings.com.

Swedish History Museum, "Odin: The One-Eyed Father." Historiska. https://historiska.se.

Noah Tetzner, "Valhalla: How Viking Belief in a Glorious Afterlife Empowered Warriors," History, March 3, 2021. www.history.com.

Websites

Life in Norway
www.lifeinnorway.net
This online guide to Norwegian life, culture, and history includes links to many articles about Norse mythology. The site includes articles about the World Tree, the gods and goddesses, and the heroes and villains of Norse mythology.

Norse Mythology for Smart People
https://norse-mythology.org
Created by Daniel McCoy, a noted scholar of Norse myths and folklore, this extremely valuable site contains a rounded, detailed look at the Norse myths, with numerous links to supportive articles, including ones on the various Norse gods, Norse cosmology, Viking culture, and diverse Norse writings.

Viking-Age History, Hurstwic
www.hurstwic.com/history/text/history.htm
Independent American scholar William R. Short, widely known as a leading expert on Norse culture, and especially Viking warfare, oversees this fact-filled website. It includes numerous links not only to the Norse myths but also to Viking daily life, ships, arms and armor, language, and much more.

INDEX

PICTURE CREDITS

Cover: Bridgeman Images

6: Maury Aaseng
9: Rawpixel.com/Shutterstock
10: Tomislav Vujnović/Alamy Stock Photo
15: Charles Walker Collection/Alamy Stock Photo
17: Science History Images/Alamy Stock Photo
23: Ivy Close Images/Alamy Stock Photo
26: Heritage Image Partnership Ltd/Alamy Stock Photo
28: Lebrecht History/Bridgeman Images
34: © Look and Learn/Bridgeman Images
37: © NPL-DeA Picture Library/Bridgeman Images
41: Prisma/Newscom
43: Chronicle/Alamy Stock Photo
46: © Look and Learn/Bridgeman Images
50: Hans Makart/Heritage Art/Heritage Images AiWire/Newscom
52: Chronicle/Alamy Stock Photo

ABOUT THE AUTHOR

Classical historian and award-winning author Don Nardo has written numerous acclaimed volumes about ancient civilizations and peoples. They include more than four dozen overviews of the mythologies of the Sumerians, Babylonians, Egyptians, Greeks, Romans, Persians, Celts, Chinese, Aztecs, Hindus, Native Americans, and others. Nardo, who also composes and arranges orchestral music, lives with his wife, Christine, in Massachusetts.